Productive
Meetings

Every Time...Guaranteed!

7· 3· 1· Fast· Track· Thinking

John Krubski

ItlcINSIGHTS Publishing

ISBN 978-0-692-63765-4

Published by

itlcINSIGHTS LLC
8 Hitchcock Road
Westport, CT 06880

For information about this title or other Fast Track Thinking
books please visit our website at: fasttrackthinking.com

*This book is dedicated to everyone who has sat through one
of "those" meetings and wondered if there wasn't a better
way to do this.*

*Also to Joanie, Ally, and Matt – who always deserve a
dedication in my book.*

CONTENTS

FOREWORD

My stock in trade is high-performance / high-productivity thinking. I put a lot of energy into elevating the thinking processes of my clients. It has worked exceptionally well for them and for me for more than 25 years.

One thing has become clear to me after years of interacting with business leaders. Better thinking is invariably the road to better leadership — even if not all leaders are better thinkers.

What's the secret that makes it possible for one person to size up a situation in seconds while others seem to wander around looking for a place to start hoping for some magic formula that will lead them to *actionable, faster thinking*?

I have come to understand that there actually is such a formula. I have made it happen for my clients and I can make it happen for you.

Over the course of more than two decades in the *real world* of corporate and creative strategic planning, it has been my experience that thinking on a higher, more practical and actionable plane is very much a learnable skill.

Drawing on decades of experience empowering executives and small business people to think more productively, paired with some of the latest academic research, numerous first-hand examples of rapid success, and much reflection, I have defined a revolutionary process called *Fast Track Thinking*. *FTT* is a new way to tackle information, distill it into highly creative and *actionable insights*, and succinctly communicate those insights to *incite the actions of others or yourself* and turn thinking into reality.

FTT is an eminently teachable and easily learnable way to significantly improve how you think without years of training or academic rigor. Fast Track Thinking can be applied at work, in school, or at home – individually and in groups – to virtually any situation where cracking the code of an issue, getting to the heart of the matter, and going from too much information to just enough to move you from thinking to meaningful, effective action.

The real problem is not how to manage the flow of information but how to make sense of information. How do we make sure we have the information we need when we need it in a form that lets us make something positive and powerful happen for us and or our organization?

This book—*Productive Meetings Every Time… Guaranteed!*—is the first of three volumes on the subject of Fast Track Thinking. Its purpose is to unleash the power of Fast Track Thinking where you might need it most immediately and most frequently—as an antidote, cure, and inoculation against that vilest of time wasters and energy dissipaters, the endless meetings you find yourself attending in your personal, professional, and community life.

There is virtually unanimous agreement and loads of research that says, when it comes to meetings, less would definitely lead to more—more time, more positive energy, more productivity. This book provides a functional code for cracking *hyper information* in meetings; along with the step-by-step process to make it work for you…fast!

This book and FTT are meant for people who attend meetings (which is most of us) as well as for people who run these meetings. After all, if the people who run meetings ran them more effectively, everyone would benefit!

For more on the future of Fast Track Thinking series, please refer to the final section of this book.

Welcome to the Hyper Information Age. Welcome to the era of Fast Track Thinking. Buckle in. Sit back. Enjoy the Ride!

John Krubski
Westport, CT

HOW THIS BOOK CAN HELP YOU

First of all, this book was written by one of the most impatient meeting-goers in the history of mankind. I am the most impatient guy in any meeting and I can't stand it when people say "This is very complicated." That kind of thinking automatically makes meetings infinitely less likely to be successful and more likely to be pointless, unproductive, even counter-productive in the end.

In my opinion, there is no such thing as too much information and even the most complicated issue can be whittled down to its fundamentals if you just use the right whittling device and know the best techniques for *idea whittling*. It's starts with cracking the code and getting to the heart of the matter...any matter.

There is a parallel between making sense of information and carving objects from wood or stone as some ancient cultures approached it. There's a story about a Polynesian man who carved a totem pole without having had any training nor previously demonstrated aptitude as a carver. When he was asked how he pulled off such a beautiful piece of work, he answered "I looked at the wood and carved away everything that was not the totem."

In the same way, taking away what isn't the meeting tends to get you right to the heart of a meeting; not only making the meeting more productive but also shorter and more actionable.

The purpose of this book is to help you make sense of meetings as an attendee or as the organizer responsible for ensuring that others makes sense of them.

What follows is a roadmap for productive, actionable meeting results. This guide does more than simply manage your time in meetings or help you organize meeting agendas or better manage the participants.

This book is about the reason we have meetings in the first place—to impart and receive, or to share and collectively take action on information.

The core of every meeting is to do something with information in a group setting. At the very least, that should be effectively communicating the information in an understandable form. At its best, a successful meeting will deliver information that improves the situation of the attendees and leads to changing the way they view and understand that situation. It may even change the way they act in that situation.

Some of you may want to rush to the *how to* section as soon as possible. If that is your unalterable predilection, have at it.

6

However, I would like you to consider reading the chapters that lead up to the *how* and *why* Fast Track Thinking works. I believe it will significantly help you make Fast Track Thinking a part of your everyday planning and the most productive and gratifying strategy for getting the most from the inevitable meetings on your schedule.

Thanks in advance

MY PROMISE TO YOU

In writing this book it is my purpose and my hope to leave you with three actionable deliverables.

1. Provide you with a code-breaking key that lets you get to the heart of any meeting— fast—without having to depend on what the meeting organizer does or fails to do.

2. As a meeting attendee—help you build a platform for getting the most value out of any meeting you attend. And as a meeting organizer—to give you the tools to make your meetings more focused and, meaningful to the attendees. And ultimately more actionable and enjoyable for everyone.

3. Give you the skills to master any amount of information under any circumstances with confidence with the certain knowledge that you will always be able to extract exactly what you need when you need it.

I hope that this little book will teach you things about meetings you don't yet know, change your mind about what you believe about meetings, and provide an energizing, stimulating and practical new way of thinking. Think of it as an *app for your brain* that helps your thinking in much the same way that programs, subroutines, and apps facilitate artificial intelligence.

If you stick with the program, and with the principles, practices, and applications FTT, I can promise you a number of valuable things:

- You will learn and understand things you would never otherwise have been able to grasp.

- You will be able to articulate those insights so cogently, eloquently, and crisply that you will be able to make sense of them for yourself and for others.

- You will be able to communicate to others what you have *figured out,* so that they will see you for the natural leader you have become.

- Best of all, internalizing Fast Track Thinking will make dealing with massive amounts of information not only non-threatening but also much more fun than you ever imagined possible.

A BRIEF HISTORY OF MEETINGS

For most of human history, only *very important people* enjoyed the privilege of attending meetings. Those meetings served *very important purposes* and were generally held for very specific...and of course *very special reasons.*

There were tribal councils to decide how the tribe would get along with itself. There were war councils to decide how the tribe would play well with others...or not. There were also spiritual councils to decide how the tribe would deal with things it couldn't see or understand but which were deemed of inestimable importance.

Later on, councils of commerce were invented where rich merchants could meet to figure out how to become richer merchants.

Then, somewhere along the line, the ultimate regularly-scheduled and monumentally unproductive meeting was invented. This was the daily ritualistic meeting of the king's court. It was also the first and prime example of meetings created for the singular purpose of having a meeting.

Meetings of the court were largely attended by people who didn't have a role or a purpose for being there — except that not attending carried some pretty heavy consequences like beheading. This monument to poor time management was responsible for introducing some of the oddest and least productive group activities ever invented.

Those activities included watching the monarch bathe, being addressed by a batch of *very special* and *very important* personages and otherwise engaging in seemingly endless, absolutely purposeless conversation which most attendees couldn't hear and many couldn't even understand.

Perhaps the greatest single contribution of the King's Court was the creation of an event at which the largest number of participants could be squeezed into a room for no apparent purpose other than to stand around and wait for something to happen...or not. Then they would disband for dinner, only to repeat it all again the next morning.

This ultimate waste of time was, thankfully, the primary job of people who could, literally, afford to do nothing meaningful all or most of the time.

People who actually worked for a living were neither invited nor required so they were free to toil in the fields, fight in the armies, and do other truly productive work to benefit the idle rich in their interminable silly meetings.

It wasn't until the modern era that the democratization of meetings drew thousands, millions, and eventually hundreds of millions of average people into the trap of unproductive meetings.

The amount of time and energy devoted to sitting together without tangible benefit or result has increased exponentially in modern times. The ability to make sense of all these engagements has not.

WHY MEETINGS ARE UNPRODUCTIVE

1. 92% of meeting attendees multitask (do not pay attention) during meetings
2. 91% of meeting attendees admit to daydreaming
3. Most professionals attend about 62 meetings monthly
4. At least 50% of meeting time is considered a waste of time
5. More than $37 billion per year is spent on unproductive meetings
6. Thre are more than 25 millon meetings every day in the United States alone
7. There are an estimated 7 billion meetings yearly in America (*SEVEN BILLION!*)
8. 15% of most organizations' collective time is spent in meetings
9. Middle managers spend 35% of their time in meetings
10. Upper management spends 50% of their time in meetings
11. People spend up to 4 hours per week preparing for status update meetings
12. Executives consider more than 67% of meetings to be failures

13. 73% of attendees admit to bringing other work into meeting times

14. 39% of attendees admit to dozing during meetings

15. One hour in a bad meeting can cost four hours in lost productivity

16. The average employee spends nearly a working week each month in unproductive meetings (31 hours)

17. 45% of attendees feel overwhelmed by the number of meetings attended

18. Universally, the most valued part of conventions and conferences is the one-on-one networking (in spite of the fact that every such conference has a "wealth" of "valuable" meetings and presentations)

19. Clearly, most people putting on meetings don't understand what they're trying to say well enough to be brief

20. Neuro scientists recognize that we have a limited amount of what they call *executive cognitive resources*; which means every minute spent in an unproductive meeting takes its toll on the quality of decision-making—both in that meeting and throughout the balance of the workday.

21. 37% of meetings are considered poorly run or unnecessary

22. 96% of workers miss at least some of the meetings they are supposed to attend—with no apparent reduction in their knowledge, understanding, productivity or status

23. 47% say meetings are the number one time waster in the office

24. Unproductive meetings increase the time you need to stay at work, making the 40-hour workweek a thing of the past

25. 45 percent of senior executives surveyed said that their employees would be more productive if their firms banned meetings for a least one-day per week

26. "Meetings are indispensable when you don't want to do anything." – John Kenneth Galbraith

27. "A meeting consists of a group of people who have little to say - until after the meeting." — *P.K. Shaw*

The disenchantment with meetings is universal, extensive and consistent. Now, you have pretty much the whole body of knowledge on that subject.

WHY DO WE EVEN BOTHER?

To begin with, we attend meetings because we just don't have anything better to replace them. In the 1982 movie *An Officer and a Gentleman*, Richard Gere plays a naval aviation cadet struggling through the rigorous training. Nearly beaten and on the verge of quitting, Gere's character eventually admits to his drill instructor in a scene at once touching and wrenching that he can't leave the program because "I got nowhere else to go!"

When it comes to meeting attendance, we apparently face the same inevitability.

But we actually have more choices than Gere's character in the movie. To begin with, we are dealing with three kinds of meetings.

There are meetings we have to attend because they're part of the system and because the organizers are as compelled to put on the meetings as we are to sit through them. Whether we get anything meaningful out of such meetings is entirely up to us.

There are also meetings that should never happen — but do happen — regularly and endlessly. Why? Because no one knows how to stop them from happening and everyone is equally fearful of what might happen if there are no meetings.

In that sense, meetings are like a pain to which we have become so accustomed that we can't conceive of life without the pain...even as we realize that chronic pain is neither good nor necessary.

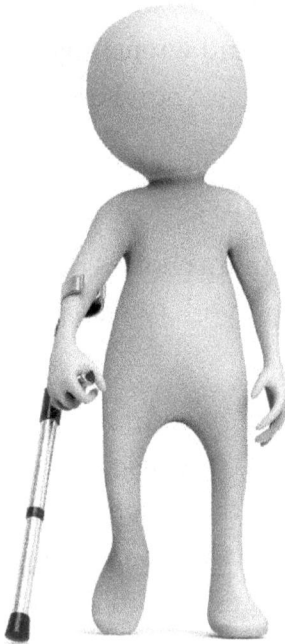

Finally, there are the meetings we want to attend — and there's the conundrum. How do we know which meetings are going to be the ones we want to attend, when there is so much evidence pointing to the probability that any meeting we do attend will disappoint?

To solve this dilemma, the singular, most important strategy is to take charge of your time, crack the code so you know what you want to learn from the meeting, and use these tools to maximize the value of the information you extract from any meeting in which you find yourself.

Welcome to the world of Fast Track Thinking!

THE PROBLEM WITH THE USUAL SOLUTIONS

So, if everybody recognizes that most meetings could be more productive, and that this insight has been around for as long as meetings have been known to suck — then why are we still wasting so much time and energy in meetings that accomplish little or nothing?

Aside from the fact that we meet because we don't know what else to do — the primary reason is that most *helpful hints for better meetings* miss the mark. They do not noticeably improve the quality of meetings.

Suggestions and strategies for *better* meetings fall into three general categories:

1. Time Management Suggestions

2. Process Management Suggestions

3. Participant Management Suggestions

Unfortunately, the simple truth is that managing time, process, and participants are exercises more akin to rearranging deck chairs on a sinking ocean liner than applying a meaningful solution to the real problem with meetings.

There is nothing inherently wrong with any of these suggestions... but then again, there's little that's right. Especially if you're looking for a solution that addresses the root cause of the problem.

That's because the real problem is not about managing the workings of the meeting or its participants. The real solution to ensure more productive meetings is making sense of information...and doing it fast.

The problem with each of these approaches is that they are, or should be, self-evident and blatantly obvious to anyone putting together or participating in meetings. If they had done the trick after all this time and since the solutions they propose are obvious to anyone who pays attention, we wouldn't still be having this conversation.

Let's review the usual solutions before we go down a wholly new road to making every meeting more productive.

The next few pages are the result of a synthesis of what's out there from the best minds, the best sources, and the most common points of view on this subject. Here also, the themes are consistent, repetitive, and predictable. Nonetheless, they are presented in their collective summarized forms.

TRADITIONAL MEETING MANAGEMENT

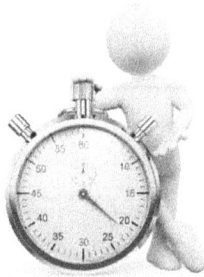

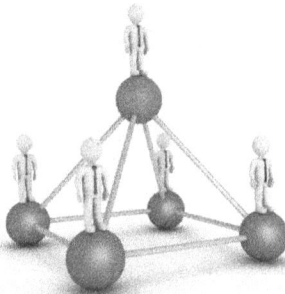

TIME MANAGEMENT SOLUTIONS

1. Don't have meetings that are unnecessary.

2. Provide the agenda and any other supporting documentation to the attendees at least 24 hours prior to the meeting time.

3. Schedule guests who don't need to be at the entire meeting, which can be an incentive to stay within the meeting's time limits.

4. Start on time. Stop on time.

5. Designate a time keeper.

6. Periodically check to see that the meeting is on time as anticipated.

7. Do not go back and review what happened before people who get there late get there.

8. Reduce the length of meetings to a maximum of one hour but try for less than half an hour.

9. Don't try to do too much in one meeting.

10. Keep Q&A to the end of the meeting.

PROCESS MANAGEMENT SOLUTIONS

1. Don't call a meeting for something that can be done better some other way.

2. Be sure everyone knows the purpose of the meeting.

3. If there is no agenda. Make one.

4. Limit action items to no more than three.

5. Have as few attendees as is absolutely necessary...preferably fewer than five.

6. No one gets to speak for more than five minutes on any one topic.

7. Don't use PowerPoint decks. Do use flipcharts.

8. Meet to support decisions. Make no decisions in the meeting.

9. Meetings should produce action plans.

10. Table any items not relevant to the agenda

11. There needs to be a meeting summary and action plan generated within 72 hours of the meeting.

12. The organizer needs to follow up with attendees to see that everyone understands their part and whether a subsequent meeting is required.

PARTICIPANT MANAGEMENT SOLUTIONS

1. Make sure everyone is adequately prepared for the meeting.

2. Don't invite people who are not necessary.

3. Have as few attendees as is absolutely necessary.

4. Keep everyone focused and on track in the meeting.

5. Give attendees 20-minute breaks every 90 minutes.

6. Reward the people who showed up on time.

7. Don't let anyone join the meeting after fifteen minutes.

8. Don't let participants hijack the conversation.

9. Allow no electronic devices.

10. Eject anyone who is doing something else in the meeting.

11. Shut down people who keep repeating what they already said or what someone else has said before.

12. Satisfy participants that a sensible process is being followed.

You now have as comprehensive a compendium of state-of-the-art information on holding better meetings as you will find anywhere.

You could probably read a hundred books (and there literally are hundreds of books on the subject of holding better meetings) along with every one of the web search hits (about 127 MILLION on Google in response to "better more effective meetings") and the list wouldn't change much, nor would it get meaningfully longer.

That means either everyone who writes on the subject is just repeating what others have already said or the fundamental principles for "better" meetings are as advanced as they ever will be and equally universal.

Considering all the money lost on unproductive meetings and all the time and energy devoted to their improvement, this seems a rather poor return.

Clearly there must be a better way to turn the time we spend in meetings into productive time, useful time, and — may we even dare hope for — more *enjoyable* time?

To get there, we need to re-think our fundamental perspective on meetings — what they're supposed to achieve *for us*, what we are supposed to take away from the meeting, and what we are supposed to do as a result of the meeting.

As you have probably figured out after reading this far—this book is not about meetings or how to run meetings. Although, the previous chapters summarize pretty much everything there is "out there" about what's wrong with meetings and the conventional ways of *fixing* those flaws.

This book is about thinking—and specifically about a very special type of thinking that can help you to get the most out of any meeting—no matter how or by whom it is being run. It's about *cracking the code* to get to the heart of the information being provided in any meeting. And doing it extraordinarily fast. It's about *Fast Track Thinking*.

Before we get to the art, science, and practice of Fast Track Thinking and how it can work for you as a meeting attendee or as a meeting organizer, let's take a step back and give a little thought to what meetings are supposed to do for you rather than what you are supposed to do with or in meetings.

YOUR MEETING BILL OF RIGHTS

Let's review what you are entitled to get from any successful and productive meeting.

First, you are the one who must either choose to waste your time in pointless meetings or to take control. You are the only person who can take the necessary steps to extract the greatest value from any meeting in the shortest possible time and with the least amount of frustration and work on your part.

In return for enduring the agony of the *meeting-damned*, you should insist on and get something of value in return. It may seem like too much to hope for, but if you expect to get nothing from a meeting…that is exactly what you are most likely to receive for your time and effort.

What follows are basic guidelines and expectations for which you should hold the meeting and its organizer accountable.

WHAT YOU SHOULD EXPECT FROM A MEETING

We're not here to fill up a room. We are here to make sense of something – in a perfect world to do that collectively and at the very least to do it individually.

BREVITY

The meeting organizer shows evidence of having made the appropriate effort to understand and communicate this topic well enough to be brief. That means the organizer should be the one person in the room who clearly understands why I am here and the one who carries the burden of conveying that understanding in as few words as possible and no more than necessary.

FOCUS

The meeting organizer is clear about the central operating principle of this meeting. At the core of every successful meeting there lies a singular rationale for that meeting – or so it should be. Every meeting has a central operating principle. I deserve to hear that principle directly from the organizer at the outset.

ACTIONABILITY

The meeting organizer is clear about what I can do and should do with what I'm getting. If the meeting is solely about providing information—that can be done far more efficiently in writing. There's no point in having everyone in the same room to have read to them what could just as easily have been transmitted in print or in bytes. The singular question of the meeting should be—*What am I supposed to do with this or about this?* It is the organizer's burden to clarify and communicate the answer to this question.

CLARITY

The meeting organizer presents the information in a form that I can readily follow and understand. The meeting organizer is the guide on a journey. It is the organizer's job to lay out a route I can readily follow.

SIGNIFICANCE

The meeting organizer provides a clear rationale of why this meeting should matter to me. It is not my job to figure out whether or not and why and how this meeting ranks on my scale of what matters most to me and to the organization. Good meetings should leave me with a strong feeling of urgency and a clear appreciation of priority. Poor meetings do neither.

EVIDENCE

The meeting organizer provides me with neither more nor less information than I need to value this meeting. The meeting organizer needs to avoid presenting too little meaningful information for me to consider important or too much information for me to make sense of.

CONCLUSIONS

The meeting organizer has taken me on a clear path from facts and data to information to insights to implications to a decision path. Meetings should follow the same progression as a logical argument (which is what they essentially are). It is the meeting organizer's responsibility to provide a logical progression from the raw material I need to know to the inevitable conclusions I should draw from that material in a logical, forward-moving manner.

If, as a meeting attendee, you have the right to these reasonable expectations, whose job is it to ensure that you get what you deserve?

Taking into consideration the fact that most meetings are unproductive and that most solutions for more productive meetings haven't achieved that much over the years, the answer to that question is crystal clear. It's YOUR job.

If you can't get them from the organizer (and generally you can't) then it's up to you to extract what matters most from the meeting. When you can make sense of the information presented in a meeting you can be sure it becomes a productive meeting – if not for everyone else, at least for you.

Now, it's time to talk about how that's going to happen...or how that's not going to happen. When you sit through a meeting, the most important thing you can take away from that meeting is not the way it was run but how much sense the meeting made.

Making sense of information is the singularly most useful meeting take-way there is.

FTT: THE NEW SOLUTION

Making Sense of Information

Making sense of information requires that you evaluate, analyze, internalize, and actualize in the meeting. That means getting to the point of the gathering while you are still in that meeting!

As the great philosopher, Yogi Berra, once said: "If you don't know where you're going, then any road will get you there." Every productive meeting should have a clear destination in mind for you. If the organizer fails to lay out both the destination and the map for getting there, then it's up to the attendees to figure that out for themselves...or not.

The key to figuring out the essence of any meeting is to put yourself into actionable *insighting* mode. Don't focus on everything coming your way. Look instead for the key "markers" (insights) that not only point the way but also help to explain the purpose of your information journey.

Consider how valuable it would be for you to make sense of the information presented in every meeting you attend before you even leave the room. To make that happen, turn your Meeting Bill of Rights into a progressive roadmap of Actionable Insighting.

We'll cover the nuts and bolts of how to make meetings productive every time for yourself in subsequent chapters. First, let's lay out some principles and foundations that underlie and define actionable steps.

Let's start with the connection between the meeting bill of rights and the path of Actionable Insighting.

1. *Brevity* is — or should be — the guiding principle for every meeting. In this case it's not just about taking the least possible amount of time, but rather about providing just enough information in the most succinct form possible. There's a great story about a letter written at great length from one past-century author to another. After going on for several pages, the writer of the letter apologizes to his correspondent: "I apologize for the length of this missive but I am of insufficient grasp of this material to be brief." Basically, the fewer words, paragraphs, or pages you can use to remind yourself of the purpose of the meeting, the better.

2. *Focus* is the key to cracking the code and getting to the heart of the meeting. Every productive meeting needs a good COP (Central Operating Principle). A COP is why the meeting is happening and what it is ultimately supposed to guide the attendees to do.

3. Which brings us to the third thing that decides whether a meeting is productive—*Actionability*. There are more than enough opinions out there about how informational meetings don't need to happen in the first place. Putting information "out there" is better handled in other formats such as emails, printed form, or in the case of progressive companies—videos. Meetings should be reserved for those occasions when people who attend them are expected at some point to DO something as a result of that meeting.

4. While brevity is at the top of the hierarchy for productive meetings, its close relative, *Clarity*, is equally important. Think of these key questions to ask when considering clarity: a) Can I follow the logic of the presentation and, if not, can I create a logic that makes sense to me? b) As the meeting unfolds, can I discern and articulate to myself what will be expected of me as a result of this meeting,

and c) Am I able to explain to someone else (in brief) what was conveyed and what my expected response to this meeting is?

5. What is the *Significance* of the information from the meeting? Can I answer the question: Why does any of this matter – to me, to the company, to anyone?

6. Can I discern and articulate what is important for me to know and what has a bearing on what I am supposed to do. What would I need to convey to somebody else so they might understand where the conclusions and the calls for action "come from?"

7. Can I walk out of the room with a simple rationale for everything? Something that I might use in answer to the question, "What was that all about?"

MAKE SENSE OF INFORMATION IN THE MEETING

While creating notes of your own or eventually getting an official post-meeting summary generated by the organizer are certainly useful things, they often miss the fundamental essence of productive meetings.

In productive meetings, everyone in the room "gets" the point and is energized and prepared for action right there in the room. The collective energy begins to dissipate the instant the meeting is over.

This is one reason meeting organizers usually save Q&A for the end of the meeting. Although, in my experience, most question periods are left to the end of the meeting where there is often too little time remaining for meaningful dialog. I often wonder if agendas designed with questions as part of the finale are really cover for inadequately prepared organizers and presenters.

Think about how different the world might have been if some of history's most famous meetings had followed today's common formats.

What do you think might have happened if John Paul Jones had ended his famous "I have not yet begun to fight!" speech by exhorting his crew to "… please review your notes and the post-meeting summary you'll get tomorrow afternoon and let me know what you think."

In a nutshell, productive collective action is a lot more likely to follow when it results from productive collective *insighting*. And that happens best while everybody is still in the room

At the very least, it will most likely happen for you when your thinking crystallizes while you are still in the session.

In the 1984 motion picture *Amadeus*, about the unusual life of composer Wolfgang Amadeus Mozart—there is a perfect moment of irony when, after hearing one of Mozart's breathtaking compositions, the Austrian Emperor (who fancies himself an accomplished musician) tells Mozart that his piece simply has "too many notes".

The same can be said of the average meeting-goer's note books. I have friends who have dozens, if not hundreds, of notebooks absolutely chock full of notes from an equally astonishing number of meetings. Yet, when asked about a particular meeting or a particular idea from those meetings they are unable to recall the information without poring over pages of notes to uncover where that precious insight might be hiding.

In my experience, taking extensive notes in meetings precisely lives down to Socrates' worst expectations of writing in general.

Socrates believed that writing things down meant what you heard ended up on paper instead of in your brain. While that idea seems quaint and misguided, Socrates may have been onto something.

Things written down end up on an external storage device (a notebook) instead of making their way into your internal hard drive (*your brain*) and into your central processor (*your thinking*).

In the same way that data on external drives is not always available to the central processor, notes put what you learn somewhere other than right there in your brain.

More than two thousand years ago, the crafty Greek philosopher may have gotten this right — what you write down may well remain outside of what you need to do good thinking. Which is why *old fashioned* and *archaic* teaching processes relied significantly on memorization of relevant and significant facts.

Having had the great benefit of a Jesuit education, I have to admit a decided prejudice in favor of sticking things into my brain regardless of whether I understand their value at the moment or not.

My memorization training has stood me in very good stead over the years and on countless occasions proven the value of my Jesuit teachers' admonition: "Learn this, Krubski. It will come in handy someday whether you appreciate it right now or not." It has more times than I can count.

In a small concession, please note that had not Socrates' students written down what he said, those bits of insight and wisdom would have gone the way of folklore.

NOTES—THE GOOD, THE BAD & THE UGLY

Here are some thoughts on the subject of taking notes in meetings.

- Most meeting notes are more like transcriptions – a comprehensive and dutiful record of everything said in the meeting. Perfectly useful as a record of the meeting, but of little use as an aid to understanding.

- You can't think while you're busy transcribing. Court stenographers capture everything, but don't necessarily process anything.

- Comprehensive notes can take as long to read as the meeting that generated them.

- It's not about keeping track of what happened in the meeting for later review. It is about using notes in the meeting to generate a better understanding of what is happening in the meeting. They are not reminders, but rather recorded instances of awareness.

- You cannot write everything down because that is like taking so many pictures of your life that you need another whole life to view them.

- Compiling an extensive library of meeting notes does not necessarily correlate with making sense of the meetings that generated them.

- Having and referring to extensive meeting notes can be like reliving every bad meeting over and over again... and who wants that?

THE POWER OF THINKING OUT LOUD

There is one great benefit to taking notes in a meeting (provided that it's done right) — notes can be the equivalent of *thinking out loud*. We generally don't view thinking out loud as a positive thing because we feel we shouldn't speak up until we have thought things through.

Nothing could be farther from the truth. Because of the way we learn and the way our brains function when we think, a wonderful and powerfully productive thing happens when we get our thoughts out of our brains where we can observe them, examine them, and evaluate our thoughts as if they were tangible, even solid three-dimensional, things.

Have you ever noticed that photographs of Albert Einstein frequently find him in front of a blackboard with the long version of his famous e=mc² formula as backdrop?

How many times have you watched television programs or movies about crime investigators only to find them standing in front of a wall of evidence, suspects, connections, insights, etc?

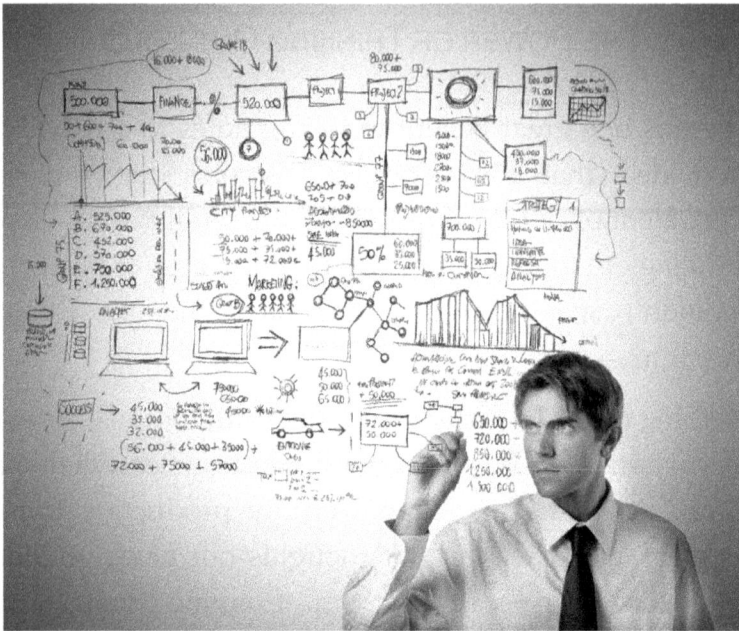

It doesn't take long to look at this recurring evidence of how some of the best thinkers think before it becomes obvious that productive thinking needs to be something that takes place outside of your brain as much as inside. Even you, the thinker, can't be sure of what's happening between your ears unless you are able to get it out in the open where you can touch it, feel it, and play with it.

Besides, when we say to someone, "I'm going to have to think about that," how are they ever to know we actually mean it unless there's some way to demonstrate the process?

Thinking out loud is an excellent way of organizing and evolving the way we think about something for ourselves. It is even more valuable when we try to communicate our thinking to someone else.

That is one reason why mathematics is often considered to be the universal language. Formulas such as $A + B = C$ are actually a symbolic way of saying that "something new is created when you combine two things that are not the same."

The formula is completely indifferent as to what A, B, and C might be, but it's clear to just about any sensate human being that the fundamentals apply across a variety of situations with a variety of variables.

Formulas literally help you see the relationships of ideas by visualizing how they fit together. In fact, the formula helps to provide a pattern for your brain that enables it to make sense of certain kinds of information.

Making sense of information requires extracting the essentials and the purpose of what is being communicated in the moment, in the meeting, and through the process.

The human brain has an incredible capacity for and competence in making sense of things by discerning the encoded patterns in information and situations. Recognizing patterns that apply across a wide range of experiences is the core of human learning and understanding.

There are two ways to crack the information code. The first is by discerning the innate patterns and connections underlying either a stream or a mass of information that aren't inherently obvious. This is essentially an intuitive human capacity.

In the movie *A Beautiful Mind*, Russell Crowe (who plays the brilliant but troubled mathematician John Nash) tries to explain to Jennifer Connelly (who plays his wife Alicia) how his mind works. He takes her outside, points to the night sky and asks her what she sees. "Stars," she answers.

He then takes her finger and traces out at first unapparent connections between the stars to turn them into constellations and characters.

Whether the moment is real or all-Hollywood, it perfectly illustrates how some people have a natural ability to see such connections. At the same time, once the connections are pointed out to her, Alicia Nash can never again look at the sky without seeing such connections.

Intuited patterns and learned patterns are the stuff of information and the fuel of learning. To paraphrase Abraham Lincoln:

> *Some of the people see unapparent connections all of the time because they have the talent to do so. All of the people are capable of doing the same thing at some level, some of the time. And all of the people are able to perceive and make use of patterning all of the time, once they have been taught how to do it.*

Without this capability we couldn't teach one another, we couldn't even communicate with one another.

PATTERN, PATTERNS, PATTERNS

Mathematical formulas are patterns; so are words. In western languages, words are patterns of sounds which are represented by letters in the written form of the language. Words are arranged in sentence patterns consistent with the grammar of a particular language — no grammar pattern = no communication.

Books are patterned with pages, chapters, and sections...and so on. Information patterns, once learned, become so *innate* and so powerful that they can mislead us as easily as they can help us. Below is an example.

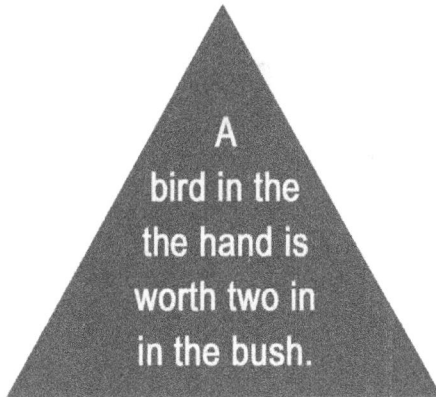

A
bird in the
the hand is
worth two in
in the bush.

A surprisingly large number of people would have missed the two instances of "in" in the above statement. We don't see the repeated word because we take for granted the pattern that prohibits it. If you were one of them, don't be concerned. Grammar patterns make it easy to read and to read without overtaxing the brain.

If you had been instructed to "edit" or "proofread" the same sentence you would most likely have caught the duplication. Finding errors in the pattern of written text such as this is why copy editors exist.

While the rest of us presume that what we read will be correct, copy editors presume that everything written is written incorrectly. We pattern for perfection. They pattern for imperfection—which is why they find typographical and grammatical errors the rest of us miss. The next time you read a book or an article and actually look for typo's, you will likely find more than you expect.

The following page is an example of how conceptual patterns work. In particular, it is an example of how strong an imposed pattern can be, unless you have the key to crack the code.

Figur471v3l7 5p34k1ng

**7H15 M3554G3
53RV35 7O PROV3
HOW OUR M1ND5 C4N
DO 4M4Z1NG 7H1NG5!
1MPR3551V3 7H1NG5!
1N 7H3 B3G1NN1NG
17 WA5 H4RD BU7
NOW, ON 7H15 LIN3
YOUR M1ND 1S
R34D1NG 17
4U7OM471C4LLY
W17H OU7 3V3N
TH1NK1NG 4BOU7 17,
B3 PROUD! ONLY
C3R741 P3OPL3 C4N
R3AD 7H15.
PL3453 FORW4RD 1F
U C4N R34D 7H15.**

If you were unable to read the above, it says:

Figuratively Speaking

**THIS MESSAGE
SERVES TO PROVE
HOW OUR MINDS CAN
DO AMAZING THINGS!
IMPRESSIVE THINGS!
IN THE BEGINNING
IT WAS HARD BUT
NOW, ON THIS LINE
YOUR MIND IS
READING IT
AUTOMATICALLY
WITHOUT EVEN
THINKING ABOUT IT,
BE PROUD! ONLY
CERTAIN PEOPLE CAN
READ THIS.
PLEASE FORWARD IF
YOU CAN READ THIS.**

Those of you who *got* this easily are exercising thinking at several levels simultaneously.

The first thing that probably happened is that you discerned the fact that the gibberish was actually words and sentences and that there was a pattern there.

In the second instance you perceived that there was a rudimentary substitution code at work here. You may or may not have been conscious of the way in which you extended normal letters to include their numerical approximates (for example the number 4 for capital A, the number 7 for capital T, and the number 1 for capital I). Once you perceived the connection, the entire page became crystal clear. This you did largely because your brain is hard-wired with the connections to intuit such patterning and approximations.

Those of you who had to work harder to make sense of the page will likely internalize the exercise, store it in your personal data bank, and apply the lesson to any similar situations in the future.

This is how and why we humans created writing in the first place.

This is also how cryptographers (code breakers) use these insights to do the work they do. This is exactly how Alan Turing (played by Benedict Cumberbatch in the movie The Imitation Game), who also happens to be the *father of modern computers*, broke the famous and presumably unbreakable Nazi Enigma code of World War II.

Turing created a huge mechanical computer into which was fed vast amounts of data from intercepts of the Nazi's coded messages. The British code breakers had only until midnight of any given day to crack the code because the German armed forces changed the code at the stroke of midnight.

Turing loaded the data into the machine and set it loose. It went ka-chunking on and on and on without a solution until Turing realized that his machine would compute for the rest of time unless it had a key to break the unbreakable code. It could compute but it needed to be told what to look for to crack the Enigma code.

The English code breakers finally realized that the answer lay in patterns that were repeated from day to day in the Nazi war machine's daily communications. At the top of the list was the frequent use of the salutation "Heil Hitler!" at the start or close of individual messages.

Turing programmed that key (along with other patterns of personal chatter used by various German encoders) into his *Bombe*. (The machine was named after the original decoding computer created years earlier by the Polish Army, who in the early 1930's laid much of the groundwork for Turing's eventual success.)

Once The Bombe had the key to making sense of the encoded German gibberish, it starting pouring out enormous masses of decoded messages that literally made it possible for the Allies to reverse the *unstoppable* advances of the Nazis and win the war in Europe.

Computers are only capable of *thinking* when they are programmed with specific instructions for how to do it and what to look for.

The foundation of Fast Track Thinking that guarantees productive meetings every time is the understanding that the way computers are programmed is essentially a way of mimicking how the human brain operates on information.

We benefit enormously when we do for our own brains what we have done for machines. FTT is an example of this process at work.

FAST, SLOW AND PROGRAMMABLE THINKING

If you have, or wish to find, the time or inclination to dig more deeply into the subject of how people think, there is a wealth of available information from a variety of intersecting disciplines including neurosciences, psychology, education theory, learning theory, and others.

The discipline of Fast Track Thinking is based on a distillation, correlation, and crystallization of what I call the applied decisional sciences — or understanding how people think so as to improve that thinking in practical circumstances — in meetings, for example.

I've boiled this body of knowledge down to a simple paradigm that says are two decisional paths when we think.

In his 2005 book (*blink*, Back Bay Books) Malcolm Gladwell does a very good job of setting up the *struggle* between *intuitive thinking* (which he calls "thin slice thinking") and *deliberative thinking* (which we would all recognize as the logical, scientific, and intensive approach favored by clinicians, researchers, and engineers).

I say the *struggle* between two decisional processes because, in his book Gladwell seems to argue in favor of the intuitive over the deliberative – a position in which he is not entirely alone.

Gladwell's argument is that *thin slice thinking* requires a very small amount of information–just enough to perceive a pattern for making decisions. He suggests that successful decisions with "just enough" evidence are correct about as often as are decisions based on extensive evidence and extended processing. In Gladwell's view decision-making "on the fly" is equally likely to be right when compared to extensively deliberated decisions.

In the course of my many years of consulting with advertising agencies, I have never ceased to marvel at the way in which creative (aka *intuitive*) people rankled at the thought of deliberative approaches to doing anything creative while the account people and clients exhibited an almost pathological disdain and even fear of anything not validated by data.

Both capacities have their upsides and their downsides. Intuitive thinking is subject to prejudices of which the thinker may be unaware but which can compromise the effectiveness of the thinking.

Deliberative thinking relies on processes and data; making it subject to fail for lack of a key piece of that data or a flaw in the thinking process.

Each road can get you to a good place...or not.

Why were we endowed with both abilities in the first place? And do they need to be mutually exclusive or combative?

I believe they are not mutually exclusive but are in fact actually two parts of a whole, ideally designed for promoting the best thinking of which we are capable.

The question is—*What does it take to harness intuition and deliberation to create a more powerful thinking engine?*

The answer to that question is *Fast Track Thinking*.

When there are two sides who are equally committed to their respective points of view, the solution often is a mediator. When two chemicals can't react spontaneously, the answer is often a third element—a catalyst.

"Mediator" and *"catalyst"* are good ways to describe the function of Fast Track Thinking.

After extensive professional experience helping creative people think more creatively and effectively and helping smart people think more intuitively, I have come to understand that there is a third way of learning. I call it *programmable thinking*—providing the brain with a *key* with which to better decode information.

Programmable thinking builds a bridge across the gulf between our intuitive side and our deliberative side.

If computer programs and *apps* mimic the way we go about thinking and in some cases make it possible f or computers to *think* instead of merely to compute, then why would it not be possible to return the favor by applying the same principles to programming the human brain for more effective thinking? Something that makes it possible for us to get more out of every information situation — and in particular the information we encounter in meetings.

Every other book you have read — or are likely to read — about attending meetings focuses on the meeting and how it is conducted. Fast Track Thinking is about making sense of the information you encounter in that meeting. This allows you to take control and determine whether a meeting is productive for you or not for yourself.

FTT: THE HOW-TO

THE FAST TRACK THINKING SOLUTION

As a meeting attendee, wouldn't it be great to have a tool to help you make sense of every meeting you attend — regardless of the skills or competence of the organizer and regardless of how well prepared for that meeting you might be? As a conference attendee, wouldn't it be great if you could get the most out of every session, every breakout, every workshop?

As a meeting organizer, wouldn't it be wonderful to be ready for any meeting, any time, on any subject even if you find out about that meeting just minutes before you are called upon to conduct it? Wouldn't it be great if you knew every attendee left every meeting you conduct fully informed and fully activated for the next steps?

I'm going to assume that your answer to each of the above questions is YES. So let's get to the heart of Fast Track Thinking and start having productive meetings every time, *guaranteed*!

AN APP FOR YOUR BRAIN

Formulas are *apps* that help frame your thinking in specific situations and help you solve problems quickly and efficiently. It is possible to create universal, dynamic apps that can improve thinking and help you make sense of large amounts of information in accelerated periods of time.

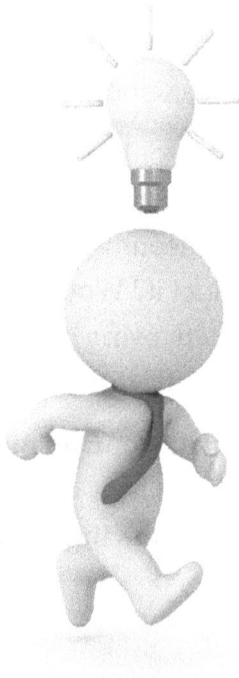

This book is about creating an app that programs the most important device you own...the one up there between the listening devices referred to as your ears.

If you were to put all of the practical experience I've gained in past 25 years, the work done in the decisional sciences, and add the fundamentals of computer programing, then shake them up until they blend, what comes out is the framework for FTT — an app that to help your brain think better, based on the following principles:

1. Machines (and brains) do their best deliberative (*computational*) work when there is something to guide them; something that narrows the parameters from infinite possibilities to manageable data and simple solutions. Turing figured that out and used it to crack the German Enigma Code.

2. A program that defines spaces for *fast thinking* within the context of definable computations is more likely to get better results than one which does not, especially if that program is framed correctly. Malcolm Gladwell, Daniel Khaneman and others understand this and have written about the interchangeability and interaction of conscious and unconscious thinking at great length.

3. The best sub-routine for your brain requires a program that minimizes the onerous heavy lifting of conscious critical thinking so as to keep your mind from being fatigued by assuming that there is too much information to process — especially if that program is framed for fast track results. This is the information overload problem mentioned earlier.

4. Many of my clients begin every project with the observation: "This is really hard." For them, it inevitably is. I begin each project with the assumption that the solution has to be simple. Because I look for such solutions within the framework of Fast Track Thinking — simple solutions abound!

FTT brings intuition, logical thinking, and programming together and provides framework for guiding focused thinking that repeatedly delivers definitive results in record time.

Every person who applies Fast Track Thinking to a meeting may come away with a different understanding — but it will be the understanding that works for them.

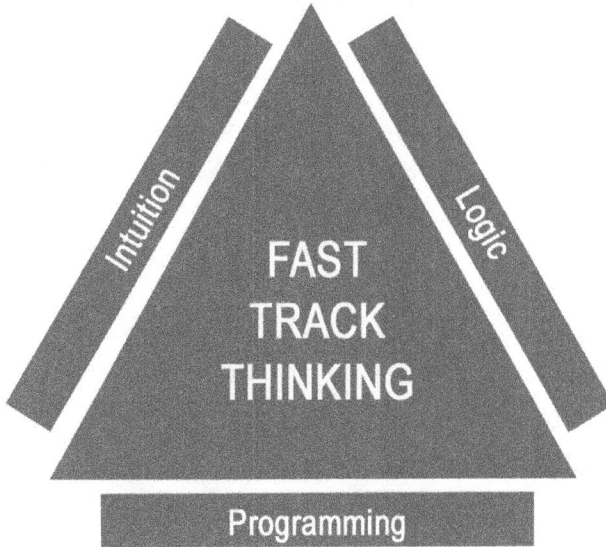

The guarantee is that each meeting attendee who uses FTT will come away with a clear, focused, and well-articulated understanding that, most importantly, is *actionable.*

That is something you can do for yourself even if meeting organizers fail to deliver on their responsibilities. FTT empowers you to do your own best thinking...brilliantly!

THINKING BY THE NUMBERS

If Fast Track Thinking is a form of programmable thinking (which it is), and programmable thinking is an *app for your brain* (which it is) then how does FTT actually work in the real world?

It all begins with THE NUMBERS. In earlier chapters, we discussed the way in which mathematics (and formulas in particular) can help to organize thinking. Formulas have always served to create a framework that combines the best of deliberative thinking while allowing room for the intuitive dynamic to express itself.

Formulas expressed externally (which I call *Thinking Out Loud*) help not only to frame the brain for more organized and productive thinking, they also tend to identify *voids* that need to be filled and connections that can be made.

Materializing these voids and connections focuses and sharpens thinking which frequently leads to the intuitive discovery of solutions.

Here how. Archimedes was an ancient Greek mathematician who had quite a challenge. The King asked Archimedes to figure out whether his new crown had been made with a cheaper combination of silver and gold instead of the pure gold the sovereign expected and had already paid for.

Archimedes' problem was a tough one— How do you measure the volume of an object with an irregular shape? Crowns certainly fall into the category of irregular shapes as each is intended to be different from all other crowns.

After working very hard on the solution, old Archimedes did what a lot of us do to relax — he climbed into a nice hot bath. As he sank deeper and deeper into the tub he noticed that every time he immersed himself, water would spill over the lip of the tub.

Archimedes suddenly jumped from the bath, naked as a new-born babe, and ran through the house crying "Eureka!" Which translates from the ancient Greek into "I have found it!"

His flash of intuition told him that you can never measure the volume of something as complex as a crown. What you can measure is the volume of water the crown displaces. *Voila* — happy king and very unhappy devious crown-maker.

Archimedes' moment of inspiration would not have meant anything if he hadn't already invented and mastered other relevant mathematical calculations and understood the principles of measuring areas and volumes.

Archimedes already had a well-earned reputation for measuring the difficult-to-measure. He was the guy who came up with a way to figure out the relationship between the circumference of a circle and its radius that makes it possible to measure the area of a circle. The *eureka experience* is a perfect example of how deliberative and intuitive thinking can work together brilliantly under the right circumstances.

The roots of Fast Track Thinking by the numbers has a similar, though less dramatic, origin.

After many years of working with one of my favorite clients (and a good friend), we had a very productive exchange.

"I've got you figured out." Frank said one day during a large group off-site meeting.

"OK, I'll bite. What do you know?" I answered.

To which Frank replied. "Every time somebody asks you a question, you get up from your chair, walk up to the front of the room and the flipchart and say, "There are three things we have to consider."

"So?" I said.

Frank looked at me as if he had just discovered some grievous transgression on my part, leaned in so we were almost nose-to-nose and said, "When you start across the room, you have no idea what those three things are, do you?" He waited triumphantly for an answer.

I had never thought about it, but I was as inspired by intuition as Archimedes might have been as I answered: "No, Frank, I don't know what those three things are — but I am one step ahead of everybody in the room because at least, I know there are three."

That moment with Frank spurred me to study my own life's work more scrupulously and with greater rigor.

Frank's question about the three things to be considered eventually evolved into a system that embraces three fundamental, and what some might call *mystical,* numbers: 7 – 3 – 1.

The purpose of what follows is to provide a method for applying FTT through *Thinking Out Loud,* so you can see how you are progressing information and to organize your active thinking while you are in the meeting room.

Finally, its purpose is to keep you from taking notes for later review and, instead, to use the Fast Track Thinking *app for your brain* so that you leave the meeting having made sense of everything said, meant, and intended.

How Fast Track Thinking Works

There are two problems we face when we process information. The first is that most people tend to over-complicate (or at the very least, over-assume the inherent complication of an information-rich situation such as a meeting).

We tend to insist that most things are far more complex than they really are. With that as a frame of reference, it is exceptionally unsurprising that things end up being complicated. Abraham Lincoln said: "If you look for the worst in people you are most likely to find it." The same goes for information. Information is only as complicated as you make it.

The second problem we face is that when we tackle a significant amount of information, we believe that we don't know where to start. Not having a place to start is a major impediment to the process of thinking—mainly because it forces us to invent a process all over again.

We hope for intuition and insight without giving ourselves even the most minimal underpinnings of process and structure to support them.

Fast Track Thinking is built around a formula for progression/reduction that can be visualized this way:

FAST TRACK THINKING

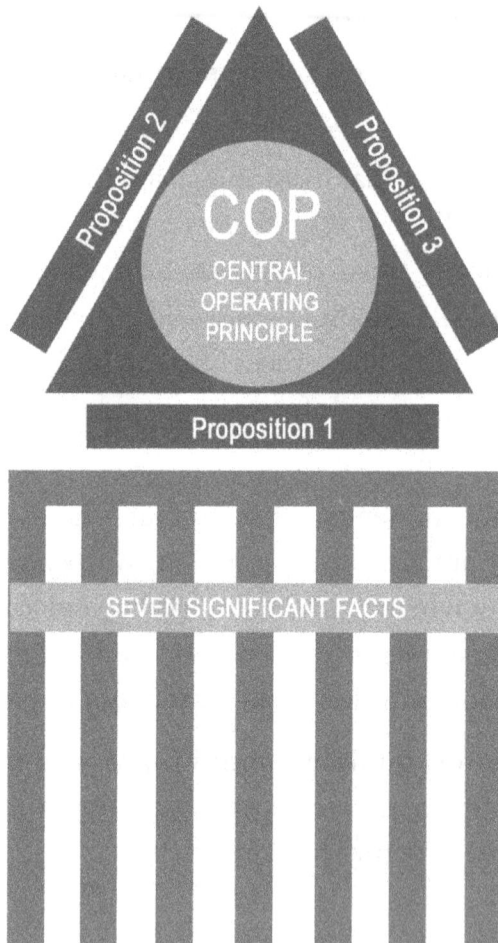

This should help to illustrate how the *mystical* numbers 7, 3, and 1 work together to build a framework for Fast Track Thinking. The goal of the framework is to progress from facts to actionable insights — no matter what the specific content or topic of a meeting.

In mathematics, 7, 3, and 1 are prime numbers, but the significance and history of these three particular numerals goes way back in time.

One is certainly the most important numeral there is, if for no other reason than it is the beginning of everything. It is also a powerful number in that it defines *The Singularity* — the only one of its kind or the absolute core of the universe.

Three, in addition to representing triangles and trinities (which have always been connected with powerful and significant dynamisms), just happens to be the smallest number of sides that can enclose a space. That is also another way of describing the minimal requirement for something that frames, limits, or otherwise delineates something.

While a circle is capable of doing the same thing, in principle, circles are impossible to meaningfully divide as they have no beginning nor end.

Seven has been a meaningful and mystical number from the dawn of time. Why is seven *lucky?* What's so special about the *seventh son of a seventh son?* The reasons may be lost in the mists of history, but the power of the number 7 has an enduring mysticism about it.

The three numbers, applied in the correct sequence, reasonably mirror the logic of thinking and communicating information.

If you make a definitive statement and someone challenges your conclusion, the odds are high that you will immediately (if you know what you're talking about that is) counter with an explanation that is instinctively framed by three rationales or propositions.

Every one of us has at one time or another begun an argument with "in the first place..." most frequently followed by a second and a third point. Consider Julius Caesar's simple logic for acquiring lands for Rome — "I came, I saw, I conquered."

Julius Caesar grew his empire on the simple principle of 3's. Winston Churchill described the defense of England during the Nazi bombardment of the Second World War during which the smaller British Air Forces defeated a much larger German air power as "Never have so many, owed so much, to so few." Clearly there is something powerful about basing an argument on three propositions.

What about *seven*? Well, to stay with the example of defending a single idea with three propositions, it is natural to assume that those propositions have to come from somewhere. Propositions are essentially conclusions and conclusions need to be based on facts.

There is much scientific research to support the conclusion that most people can remember a maximum of seven facts relative to any idea. Clearly there's no point to marshaling a longer argument list when no one will ever meaningfully embrace more than seven.

At the same time, if you have one idea, supported by three propositions, you simply can't have fewer than seven facts from which your argument is drawn. If you can't come up with seven facts that serve as the foundation of a meeting, then that meeting probably should not have been held in the first place and there is too little evidence that it has any purpose.

The role of Fast Track Thinking is to create a defined productive space for your thinking process that combines the best of intuition and logic by shaping or framing that thinking through the programming of the 7 – 3 – 1 sequence.

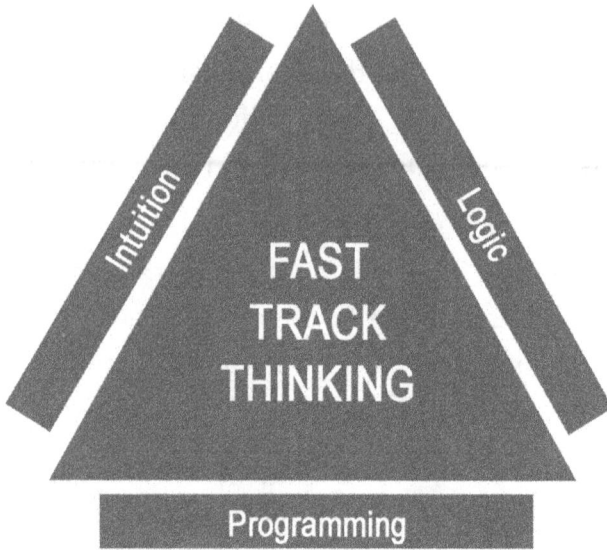

Working from the foundation up, FTT begins by identifying *seven significant facts* in the information being presented to meeting attendees.

The use of the word *significant* is intentional because it makes creates a space for intuition, as intuition is extremely important when it comes to making sense of information.

Rather than making notes on everything said in the meeting, step one is to identify the seven facts that your gut tells you are *significant* or important, or meaningful.

That is to say, your experience and intuition will tell you, "There's something here that matters somehow, even if you don't exactly yet know how it all fits together; but you just feel that this is something you need to pay attention to."

Since you only have seven factual spaces you need to fill in on this list, you'll want to be sure at the gut level that the ideas you put here matter. You can always change them as your understanding of what's significant becomes clearer.

The next two pages are a template that you can copy or print out and take to each meeting instead of relying on an open-ended notebook, pad, or sheet.

FTT In-Meeting Template—Part 1

FTT In-Meeting Template   © John Krubski 2016

One **Central** Operating Principle (What is the point of this meeting.)

Three **Concise** Propositions (Where do the facts take us?)

1.

2.

3.

Seven **Significant** Facts (What facts are vital to this meeting?)

1.

2.

3.

4.

5.

6.

7.

FTT In-Meeting Template—Part 2

Notable Information Holding Pen

Write facts about which you feel strongly on the first template page.

Park other ideas here until you feel they have value or you are prepared to discard them.

Sometimes you may only see the value of a fact after more information comes in.

Sometimes a fact will fall off as supporting information renders it of lower importance.

Sometimes you will see that several little facts point to another fact of greater significance.

You can download full-sized PDF templates at: www.fasttrackthinking.com

THE LOGIC OF FAST TRACK THINKING

What this structure does for you is simple but essential if you are to get the most from every meeting. There's no point in organizing or attending a meeting unless it has a point. As we know, organizers often don't know how to get that point across – or don't actually have a point of which they themselves are aware.

By applying the concept of Fast Track Thinking, you can leave the room with the ability to tell yourself first...and thereafter, anyone who asks the question, "What was that meeting all about?"

Envision yourself concluding meetings in the future with this kind of clarity.

- *I know that the core purpose of this meeting was...*

- *I have come to this conclusion because ...*

- *The first proposition supports and/or points to it.*

- *The second proposition supports and/or points to it.*

- *The third proposition supports and/or points to it.*

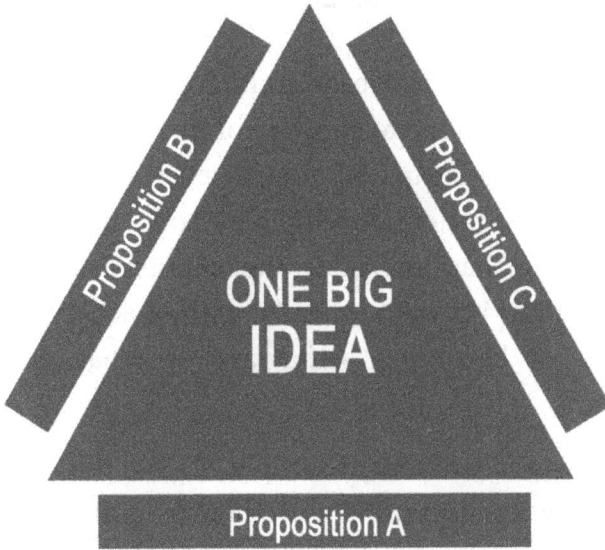

Proposition B

Proposition C

ONE BIG IDEA

Proposition A

The propositions make sense as they are based on and grounded in the following facts:

1. Significant Fact
2. Significant Fact
3. Significant Fact
4. Significant Fact
5. Significant Fact
6. Significant Fact
7. Significant Fact

FTT Example — Education

My daughter, who teaches Biology to high school freshmen, asked me to show 45 of them how to use Fast Track Thinking in an end-of-term exercise. Her goal was to have each student develop a personal understanding of what they had learned in the course of the semester. *Metacognition* is what they call it in the teacher zone — the process of becoming self-aware of what you have learned.

Here's a good summary example of what the 9th graders came up with, beginning with their 7 significant facts:

1. All life starts with a single cell.
2. Cell division is how all living things grow.
3. Living things depend on the ecosystems in which they live.
4. Evolution is how living things change to be able to adapt to changing environments.
5. Animals need some kind of central control system to keep things on track.
6. All living things need fuel to stay alive.
7. Living things are built to process and distribute fuel so that the individual cells can stay alive and healthy.

When they were asked to reduce these facts to three propositions, this is what they said they learned:

- How living things are built
- How living things work
- How living things change

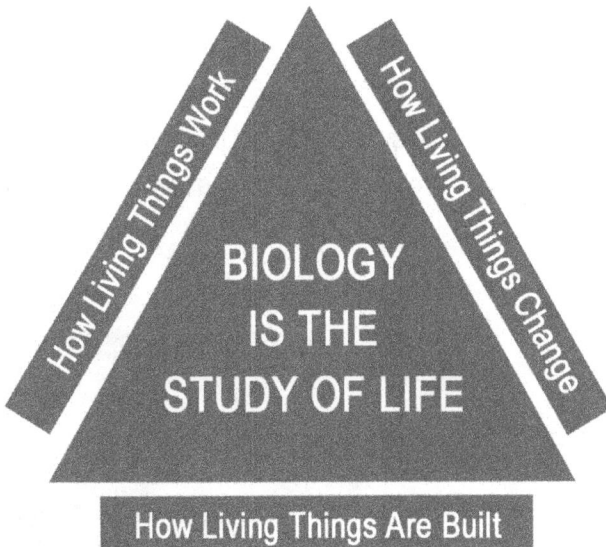

That thinking led them to understand the fundamental nature of Biology: Biology – is the study of life.

The irony is that the word *biology* itself comes from two Greek words that combine to mean exactly that. The kids did not know the origins of the word but they certainly got the idea…and entirely on their own.

FTT Example — Marketing

On another occasion, I was commissioned to help a group of advertising agency creative people charged with introducing and explaining the benefits of a different kind of fruit and make it *sexy* and special in the process.

The fruit (Cherimoya) has some interesting characteristics. It can honestly be described as *ugly* on the outside. The inside looks equally odd and pretty much resembles something that has gone bad. It also has a special delectable flavor.

Very few people know about the fruit, but those who do tend to really love its unique taste and texture — not to mention the fact that its name is as exotic as its appearance.

The seven facts we identified can be summarized as follows:

1. Looks like something left over from the age of dinosaurs — and possibly beyond that.
2. Definitely not one of the prettiest fruit you'll ever see.
3. Looks equally questionable on the inside.
4. Been around a long time, but nobody seems to know about it.
5. Tastes so good more people should know about it — provided they get beyond the appearance.
6. Once you try it, you're likely to love it.
7. In spite of the foregoing, there's nothing special you can say that doesn't apply to other fruit.

It turns out that what we were being asked to sell is a rare fruit that looks like it goes back to the dawn of time and is beloved loved by those who are lucky enough to discover it and who can see beyond the surface.

Uniquely Weird Looking

Known of by Very Few

WORTHY OF LEGEND

Adored by Its Aficionados

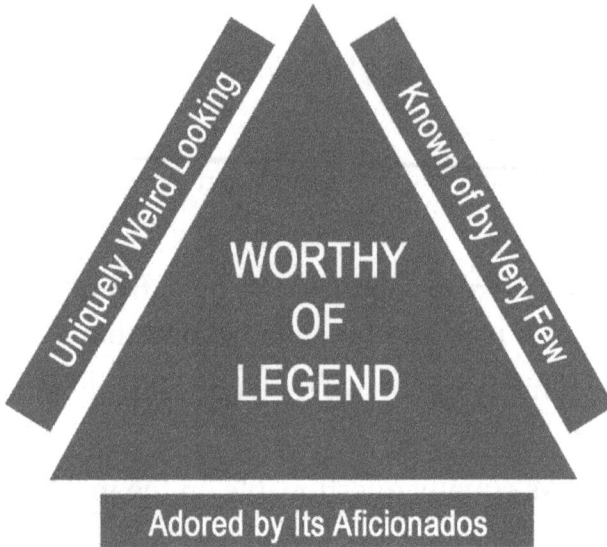

Since the assignment was to find a way of saying something original that hasn't been said about other fruit, we decided that the Central Operating Premise of Cherimoya is that it should well be "Worthy of Legend."

Clearly, there is no legend...but based on the process and the conclusions, we determined that there should be one for something as *special* as Cherimoya. In the process, we transformed the fruit from an unattractive unknown into an *intriguing should be known.*

FTT EXAMPLE — STRATEGIC PLANNING

For another *"interesting"* assignment, I was tasked with the challenge of helping a convention of waste water district managers redefine the "business they are in" and to articulate a more compelling, inspiring and energizing vision on which to reimagine their industry and attract fresh eager young talent. Oh — and all that had to happen in 90 minutes or less.

The conventional view of the people and the activity of waste water management is not all that compelling, inspiring, nor energizing. It is typically associated with un-pleasantries, unattractive machinery, and less than pleasing olfactory experiences.

The 7 significant facts about waste water aligned themselves like this:

1. Once you say you are in the *waste water* business, everything that follows is colored by less than flattering assumptions and emotions.

2. Without water there is no life.

3. Yet, fouled water can cause more harm than good.

4. Pretty much everybody lives downstream of somebody else's waste water.

5. Aside from the waste in water, there are valuable and useful things that can be recovered and reused by today's waste water managers with today's technology.

6. We make ugly water beautiful.

7. Every gallon of clean water we reclaim and put back in the system saves a gallon of clean water that we otherwise have to extract from the ecosystem.

The propositions derived from the exercise were:

- Without water there is no life.
- Clean water is a beautiful thing.
- Waste water is an ugly thing.

Which can also be expressed this way:

No Water. No Life. Clean Is Beautiful

WE MAKE LIFE POSSIBLE AND PLEASURABLE

Waste Water Is Ugly

If you were a young person considering a career decision, which version of water management constitutes the more attractive option for a career?

These examples are intended as models for applying Fast Track Thinking to information which you find yourself dealing with in meetings. Continually thinking in terms of the 7 - 3 - 1 format makes it easier to organize that information and make sense of it as you go.

FTT LETS YOU START ANYWHERE

The good thing about FTT is that you can start anywhere in the chain of thinking.

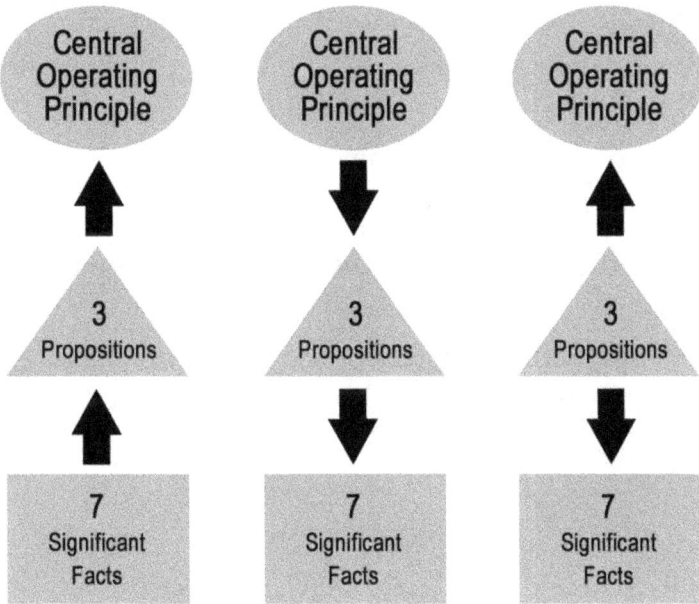

If a blinding flash of inspiration leaves you with the big idea but you need to make sense of and support—go top-down to develop the whole story.

When facing mountains of information, you need to distill into insights. Start at the bottom, develop *seven significant facts* and ladder up to the Central Operating Premise.

If you find yourself with three somehow related but non-duplicated perspectives on something, go whichever way—up or down or from the middle—is the most immediately productive.

Because the *app for your brain* keeps you focused on the logical path for making sense of information, you'll get the whole picture regardless of where you begin and in which direction (up or down) you go first.

PRACTICE MAKES PERFECT

Making sense of information is not a meetings-only activity. If you think about it, you probably have a range of potential applications for Fast Track Thinking.

You regularly access web search information. You read articles, books, magazines. You tackle reports, summaries.

No matter whether you are in school, work full-time, or spend a lot of time watching television — if you are dealing with information with which you need (or want) to deal — every such instance can benefit from FTT.

More importantly, the more you practice the process, the better it will work for you.

Don't wait to start applying Fast Track Thinking until your next meeting. Put it to work today — or tomorrow at the latest.

Don't forget to download the Fast Track Thinking templates and start today. You'll find them here:

www.fasttrackthinking.com

FTT FOR ORGANIZERS

And now.... It's time to talk about YOU, the meeting organizer. You too can be part of the solution...or not.

How would it feel to be able to walk into any meeting, on any subject, on a moment's notice and still be sure you can deliver a productive meeting to your audience?

How would it feel to see that every time you organize and run a meeting people leave with a clear understanding, a strong sense of purpose and a set of actionable insights?

How would it feel to be secure in the knowledge that attendees of your meetings are far more likely to consider those meetings well worth their while?

All you need to do is follow the Fast Track Thinking templates to organize the information for your meeting and follow the format in creating and delivering your presentation.

Yes, it is that simple!

MUCH MORE TO COME

If you like what you are beginning to learn about *Fast Track Thinking* and the world of possibilities it can afford you, there's a lot more of which you might want to be aware.

The evolving story of *Fast Track Thinking* lives at **www.fasttrackthinking.com.**

If you might be interested in some useful live applications of *Fast Track Thinking* for your company, group, association, or organization, you can find a lot of information on how the author can share, use and teach *Fast- Track Thinking* to help make your next offsite, convention, or business meeting more productive at **www.catalystspeaker.com.**

If you would like to know more about the author, John Krubski, simply Google "John Krubski" or go to **www.itlcinsights.com.**

How to get your team, group, or organization from meeting to insight to action plan in one day or less!.

Unleash the Power of Fast-Track Thinking

Fast Track
Team
Planning

7 · 3 · 1 · 3 · 7

JOHN KRUBSKI

INCLUDES THE FAST· TRACK· THINKING APP FOR YOUR BRAIN

AVAILABLE Q2 2016

How to unleash the power of Fast
Track Thinking to make what happens
next in your organization...happen!

Unleash
the Power
of
Fast-Track
Thinking

Create

The Future

Your Organization

Deserves

JOHN KRUBSKI

INCLUDES THE FAST· TRACK· THINKING APP FOR YOUR BRAIN

AVAILABLE 2017

The key to understanding Millennials is seeing them in the context of the generations that came before and will come after

Unleash
the Power
of
Fast-Track
Thinking

How
Generations
Decide

A Fast Track Thinking perspective on how to connect with each of America's six generations across the spread of their values profiles

JOHN KRUBSKI

INCLUDES THE FAST· TRACK· THINKING APP FOR YOUR BRAIN

AVAILABLE 2017

Our brains are purpose-built to deal with
enormous amounts of information rapidly...
we just forgot to let them do their job

Unleash
the Power
of
Fast-Track
Thinking

The Power of
Fast Track
Thinking

How to stop worrying about information
overload and learn to love the
Hyper Information Age

JOHN KRUBSKI

INCLUDES THE FAST· TRACK· THINKING APP FOR YOUR BRAIN

AVAILABLE 2018

A fresh look at American decisions and values
based on original research encompassing
more than 35,000 Americans

Unleash
the Power
of
Fast-Track
Thinking

How
Americans
Decide

A Fast Track Thinking perspective on
the eight different decisioning models
Americans use to guide their lives

JOHN KRUBSKI

INCLUDES THE FAST· TRACK· THINKING APP FOR YOUR BRAIN

AVAILABLE 2018

How to unleash the power of
Fast Track Thinking to make what happens
next in your life...happen

Unleash
the Power
of
Fast-Track
Thinking

Create

The Future

You

Deserve

JOHN KRUBSKI

INCLUDES THE FAST· TRACK· THINKING APP FOR YOUR BRAIN

AVAILABLE 2019